CW00602909

A GUIDE TO
MACBETH

STEVE EDDY
WITH TONY BUZAN

Hodder & Stoughton

ISBN 0 340 80226 X

First published 2001
Impression number   10 9 8 7 6 5 4 3 2 1
Year   2005 2004 2003 2002 2001

Cover photograph ©: Anthony Sher as Macbeth, copyright Donald Cooper, Photostage
Mind Maps: Ann Jones and David Orr
Illustrations: Karen Donnelly, Julian Mosedale and David Ashby

Typeset by Transet Limited, Coventry, England.
Printed in Great Britain for Hodder & Stoughton Educational, a division of
Hodder Headline Plc, 338 Euston Road, London NW1 3BH by Cox and Wyman Ltd,
Reading, Berks.

CONTENTS

MEMORY

Your magnificent 'Memory Muscle'

Your memory is like a muscle. If you don't use it, it will grow weaker and weaker, but if you do keep it exercised, it will grow stronger and stronger. Here are four tips for improving your memory:

1 **Work for between 20 and 40 minutes at a time, and then take a break.** This allows your Memory Muscle to rest and lets the information sink in.
2 **Go back over your work.** Wait for a little while after you have been learning something, and then look back at it later.
3 **Make connections.** Your Memory Muscle becomes stronger when it can link things together. Join the separate facts together in some way to make a picture, for example on a Mind Map, and they'll come back to you all together, in a flash!
4 **Think big.** Your Memory Muscle gets stronger if what it is trying to remember is special in some way, so 'think big' and make what you are learning eye-catching.

Your new magic learning formula – the Mind Map®

The Mind Map is a very special map. It helps you to find your way around a subject easily and quickly because it mirrors the way your brain works. Use it for organizing your work both at school and at home, for taking notes and planning your homework.

THE MIND MAPS IN THIS BOOK

Look at the Mind Map on p. 14. In the centre is a picture summarizing the theme of the topic. Coming out from this are several branches, each covering an important part of the topic.

HOW TO READ A MIND MAP

1 Begin in the centre, the focus of your topic.
2 The words/images attached to the centre are like chapter headings: read them next.

3 Always read out from the centre, in every direction (even on the left-hand side, where you will have to read from right to left, instead of the usual left to right).

HOW TO DRAW A MIND MAP

1 Start in the middle of the page with the page turned sideways. This gives your brain the maximum width for its thoughts.
2 Always start by drawing a small picture or symbol. Why? Because a picture is worth a thousand words to your brain. And try to use at least three colours, as colour helps your memory even more.
3 Write or draw your ideas on coloured branching lines connected to your central image. These key symbols and words are the headings for your topic.
4 Then add facts, further items and ideas by drawing more, smaller, branches on to the main branches, just like a tree.
5 Always print your word clearly on its line. Use only one word per line.
6 To link ideas and thoughts on different branches, use arrows, colours, underlining and boxes.

You see how easy it is! You have summarized an entire topic on just one page, and this is now firmly logged in your brain, for you to get at whenever you want! If you look at this Mind Map five times over the next five months, the information it contains will be in your brain for many, many years to come.

Make life easy for your brain

When you start on a new book or topic there are several things you can do to help get your brain 'on line' faster:

1 Quickly scan through the whole book or topic.
2 Think of what you already know about the subject.
3 Ask 'who?', 'what?', 'why?', 'where?', 'when?' and 'how?' questions about your topic.
4 Have another quick scan through.
5 Build up a Mind Map.
6 Mark up any difficult bits and move on.
7 Have a final scan.

And finally, have fun while you learn.

HOW TO USE THIS GUIDE

This guide will help you whether you read the whole play or just an extract of one or two key scenes – called 'Hot scenes' in this guide. It will help you to understand, enjoy and revise the play.

WHICH BITS SHOULD I READ?

Try to read the whole play and the whole guide! However, many students just read an extract from the play. This is all right, but you should at least know the full story, so you can see how the extract fits in. For this, read the guide section 'The Story of *Macbeth*'.

You will also understand the extract better if you know something about all the characters in the play. So read the 'Characters' section, focusing on characters in the extract.

Definitely read the 'Commentary' section on the extract you are studying. The 'Key ideas' and 'Style' sections take you a little deeper. The 'Word from Will' boxes give background.

The 'Model answer' shows you what a really good exam answer is like. Don't try to copy it, but read the notes on what's good about it.

The Glossary explains special words or phrases used in the guide (typed in **bold**).

QUESTIONS

In the 'Commentary' there are questions marked with a star ✪. Think about these to develop your own ideas. They do not normally have a single right answer.

At the end of each 'Hot scene' there is a 'Hotspot' with questions and activities. These will help you to develop your ideas and remember what you have learned. You could take a break *before* this, but you should certainly take one *after* the Hotspot before re-reading the scene or doing other work.

THE STORY OF *MACBETH*

ACT 1: PREDICTION

The Witches predict that Macbeth will become Thane of
Cawdor, then King, and that Banquo will be the father of kings.
The first prediction comes true when Duncan rewards Macbeth
with the title 'Thane of Cawdor'. Macbeth and his wife resolve
to kill Duncan so that Macbeth can be King.

ACT 2: MURDER

Macbeth kills Duncan, pinning the blame on Duncan's
attendants. A drunken Porter lets Macduff and Lennox into
Macbeth's castle. When the murder is discovered, Duncan's
sons Malcolm and Donaldbain flee. Macbeth becomes King.

ACT 3: AN UNINVITED GUEST

Macbeth hires murderers to kill Banquo and his son Fleance,
but Fleance escapes. Banquo's ghost terrifies Macbeth at a
banquet, and the banquet breaks up. Hecate, goddess of
witchcraft, meets the Witches. Macduff has gone to King
Edward of England to ask for help against Macbeth. Malcolm is
already there. Edward prepares for war.

ACT 4: HUBBLE, BUBBLE

The Witches show Macbeth three spirit apparitions. These tell
him to fear Macduff, but otherwise make him feel that he
cannot be defeated until Birnam Wood comes to Dunsinane –
which seems unlikely! However, they also show him that
Banquo's descendants will be kings. Macbeth has Macduff's
family murdered. Malcolm tests Macduff's loyalty by
pretending to be unfit to rule. Macduff hears that his family
have been slaughtered and vows revenge on Macbeth.

connections between events

1 Witches plan to meet Macbeth

2 Duncan hears how Macbeth and Banquo have led his army to victory

3 Witches predict Macbeth will be Thane of Cawdor, and Banquo will father a line of kings

4 Duncan makes Macbeth Thane of Cawdor and makes Malcolm heir to throne

5 Lady Macbeth persuades Macbeth to kill Duncan and he does

6 Murder discovered. Malcolm and Donalbain decide to flee

7 Macbeth has Banquo killed

8 Banquo's ghost appears at banquet

9 Witches show Macbeth apparitions

10 Macbeth has Macduff's family killed

11 Malcom tests Macduff's loyalty at English court

12 Malcom leads army to Scotland. Macbeth prepares army for battle

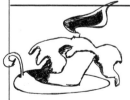

13 Lady Macbeth's madness and suicide

14 Macduff kills Macbeth in battle. Malcolm becomes King

ACT 5: BATTLE LINES

Lady Macbeth goes mad, and while Macbeth prepares for battle she kills herself. Macbeth is close to despair but is still determined to fight to the end. He loses hope of winning when he sees Birnam Wood coming towards his castle – the enemy have camouflaged themselves with branches. He leads his men into battle, and is killed by Macduff. Malcolm will now be King, restoring health and peace to Scotland.

Test yourself

Circle the right answers in the account of the story below. Then check your answers by referring back.

ACT 1: PREDICTION

The Witches predict that Macbeth will be (**late for dinner / Thane of Cawdor / Mayor**), then King, and that Banquo will be the father of kings. The first prediction comes true when Duncan rewards Macbeth with the title. Macbeth and his wife resolve to (**flatter / impress / kill**) Duncan so that Macbeth can be King.

ACT 2: MURDER

Macbeth kills Duncan, pinning the blame on Duncan's (**attendants / sons / wife**). A drunken Porter lets Macduff and Lennox into Macbeth's castle. When the murder is discovered, Duncan's sons Malcolm and Donaldbain (**fight / weep / flee**). Macbeth becomes King.

ACT 3: AN UNINVITED GUEST

Macbeth hires murderers to kill (**Banquo / Macduff / Malcolm**) and his son Fleance, but Fleance escapes. Banquo's ghost terrifies Macbeth at a banquet, and the banquet breaks up. Hecate, goddess of witchcraft, meets the Witches. Macduff has gone to King Edward of (**France / England / Norway**) to ask for help against Macbeth. Malcolm is already there. Edward prepares for war.

ACT 4: HUBBLE, BUBBLE

The Witches show Macbeth three spirit apparitions. These tell him to fear (**Malcolm / trees / Macduff**), but otherwise make him feel that he cannot be defeated until Birnam Wood comes to Dunsinane – which seems unlikely! However, they also show him that Banquo's descendants will be kings. Macbeth has Macduff's family murdered. Malcolm tests Macduff's (**loyalty / intelligence / patience**) by pretending to be unfit to rule. Macduff hears that his family have been slaughtered and vows revenge on Macbeth.

ACT 5: BATTLE LINES

Lady Macbeth goes mad, and while Macbeth prepares for battle she (**recovers / gets drunk / kills herself**). Macbeth is close to despair but is still determined to fight to the end. He loses hope of winning when he sees Birnam Wood coming towards his castle – the enemy have camouflaged themselves with branches. He leads his men into battle, and is killed by (**mistake / Macduff / a falling tree**). Malcolm will now be King, restoring health and peace to Scotland.

Macbeth

Macbeth is a **tragedy**. This is not just a play with a sad ending, but one with special rules. A tragedy has a **tragic hero**, someone noble, to be admired. Yet this person always has a fatal weakness, or makes a bad mistake. This, combined with fate, leads to the hero's downfall and death.

How can Macbeth be called a 'hero'? He's a scheming murderer and a tyrant – doesn't that make him a villain? It does, but for the play to work as a tragedy he has to be more than that – someone heroic who somehow slips towards self-destruction. Does he only have himself to blame? You decide!

BRAVE MACBETH

How is Macbeth noble? For a start he is very brave. The Captain (or 'Sergeant') in Act 1, scene 2, reports Macbeth's fierceness and courage on the battlefield. We see him as a man of action, his sword steaming with the blood of his enemies.

However, Macbeth is brave only when he knows what to do and feels no guilt. When he first thinks of murdering King Duncan (Act 1, scene 3), his hair stands on end and his heart pounds. In Act 2, scene 1, he imagines a dagger leading him to commit murder. He is horrified at what he must do. He is even afraid that the paving stones will give him away.

After the murder he is almost hysterical. Lady Macbeth has to take the daggers back to the chamber. In the banquet scene (Act 3, scene 4), he is terrified of Banquo's ghost.

BEING A 'MAN'

Macbeth likes to think of himself as a 'real man'. When he sees Banquo's ghost he insists that he would gladly fight a *rugged Russian bear*, an *armed rhinoceros* or a *Hyrcan tiger* (famously fierce!). It is just the unknown that he cannot face – that and his terrible sense of guilt. It shakes his *single state of man*. Lady Macbeth knows her husband well. When he decides not to commit the murder she persuades him to do it by calling him a coward.

CONSCIENCE VERSUS AMBITION

Macbeth starts as a loyal, honest subject, proud of the praise he gets for defending king and country, and of his new title, *Thane of Cawdor*. However, Macbeth is also an ambitious man, so when the Witches predict that he will be King, he is torn. He wants this very much, but he thinks he has to kill Duncan to make the prediction come true.

He knows that killing a king is probably the worst crime that there is. In a **soliloquy** (a solo speech) in Act 1, scene 7, he thinks hard about the reasons for not doing it. In fact he decides to go no further – until Lady Macbeth changes his mind back again. Once he has done the dreadful deed, he regrets it straight away. He calls his bloody hands *a sorry sight*. He feels his guilt has cut him off from God.

In Act 3, scene 1, he persuades himself to murder Banquo. He thinks he and Lady Macbeth will then be safe and happy. He fears Banquo's *royalty of nature*, not only because Banquo might guess his guilt, but because Banquo is such a good man.

AN IMAGINATIVE MAN

Macbeth is an imaginative man. When he first thinks of murder, he speaks of his *horrible imaginings*. He also has the imagination to think about the consequences of murder. Before the murder he imagines the floating dagger, and afterwards he hears a voice crying *Sleep no more!* Perhaps he only imagines Banquo's ghost.

Perhaps if he could be less sensitive, and less imaginative, he could commit these murders without it affecting him so badly. Lady Macbeth certainly thinks the answer is just not to think about it all so much.

ONLY HIMSELF TO BLAME?

Is Macbeth an evil man? Is he a victim of evil? He is linked to the Witches in Act 1, scene 1. What's more, the Witches do not try to lead Banquo astray as they do Macbeth. ✪ Is this because they think their job will be easier with Macbeth because he is easier to tempt?

Macbeth is over-ambitious. He is excited by the Witches' prophecy, and pleased to be made Thane of Cawdor. However, Lady Macbeth does her best to make him commit the first murder, and the Witches lead him to his own destruction by their trickery.

HOW MACBETH CHANGES

The first hint of Macbeth's dishonesty is when he pretends that he has not been thinking about the Witches (Act 2, scene 1): *I think not of them.* Gradually he becomes more and more scheming. He puts on a show of grief and anger when Duncan is found dead. He tricks some poor men into murdering Banquo. He has Macduff's family slaughtered, and he rules Scotland as a cruel tyrant.

In one important way, however, Macbeth becomes more heroic, even while behaving more and more badly. This is because he gradually takes responsibility for his own actions. He does not consult his wife before having Banquo murdered. He becomes independent of her. More than this, he realizes that there is no turning back:

I am in blood
Stepped in so far that should I wade no more,
Returning were as tedious as go o'er.

When the Witches make him think he cannot be defeated –
and yet tell him to fear Macduff, he decides to become entirely
the 'man of action', no longer prey to his own guilt. Yet on the
battlefield he still has enough conscience to try to avoid
fighting Macduff, because he has already killed Macduff's
family.

Above all, Macbeth comes to accept his fate. He realizes that
the Witches have led him into a fatal trap, but he is
determined to fight to the bitter end. ✪ Do you admire that?
What do you think about him now – villain or victim?

Lady Macbeth

In some ways Shakespeare's audience might see Lady Macbeth
as the ideal wife. She is loyal and supportive to her husband.
She encourages his ambition. She covers up for him when he
is in danger of revealing his guilt. Yet in other ways she is far
from ideal.

AN EVIL WOMAN?

Lady Macbeth first appears in Act 1, scene 5. She is reading
Macbeth's letter about the Witches. She believes
unquestioningly in the prediction, and assumes that Macbeth
must kill Duncan for it to come true. Her one worry is that
Macbeth may be too full of the *milk of human kindness.*

She feels that she must make herself strong for the job in hand.
Therefore she calls on evil spirits to *unsex* her (make her like a
man) and fill her with *direst cruelty*. Even so, she still needs a
drink to give her courage when it comes to Duncan's murder.
She also claims that she would have killed him herself – except
that he reminded her of her father. Is this just an excuse?

'JUST DON'T THINK ABOUT IT'

When not appealing to evil spirits, Lady Macbeth is very down
to earth. When Macbeth has been terrified by the ghost of

Banquo, she tells him he just needs a good night's sleep. Her way of coping with guilt is to think about it as little as possible. We see a hint of this when she appeals to Night to hide the coming murder, so that even the knife cannot see the wound it makes, and so that heaven cannot *peep* at it. She encourages Macbeth to adopt the same approach. After the murder she tells him, *Consider it not so deeply.* ❏ If you know the play, how well does this approach work?

A PERSUASIVE WOMAN

Lady Macbeth is very persuasive. She gets Macbeth to commit the murder by questioning his courage, probably knowing his insecurity. She also impresses him by saying that she would have dashed her own baby's brains out if she had sworn to do so as Macbeth has sworn to kill Duncan. She is ruthless, but she is also manipulative, because Macbeth hasn't actually sworn to murder Duncan.

SLIPPING INTO MADNESS

Lady Macbeth thinks that she and her husband can just 'wash their hands' of the murder – literally. She says, *A little water clears us of this deed.* Unfortunately for her this turns out to be far from true. Her guilt drives her mad. She walks and talks in her sleep, forever trying to wash a *damned spot* of blood from her hands (Act 5, scene 1).

In the end she becomes a pathetic, broken woman, complaining that *all the perfumes of Arabia will not sweeten this little hand.* Finally, she kills herself.

Banquo

Banquo is a good man, but how good? He is as brave as Macbeth, although Duncan does not reward him. Macbeth himself speaks of Banquo's *royalty of nature.* The Witches do not try to lure him into self-destruction, and he does not at first take them very seriously. However, they do promise that he will be the father of kings.

Banquo is wary of the predictions. He warns Macbeth that the Witches may trick him with *honest trifles.* He loses sleep over *cursed thoughts* which seem to be connected to the Witches. However, when Macbeth wants to discuss the predictions, he agrees only on the condition that he can remain loyal to Duncan, and guilt-free.

Perhaps Banquo's only real fault is that he suspects Macbeth of murdering Duncan, yet does nothing about it. ❍ Is this because he hopes to gain from the Witches' predictions himself?

Macduff

Macduff is a brave, honest man who shows no signs of personal ambition. We first meet him listening good-humouredly to the drunken Porter (Act 2, scene 3). When he discovers Duncan's murder, he is horrified, and orders the *alarum bell* to be rung.

Macduff is contrasted with Macbeth in this scene. Macbeth sounds very insincere when he tells Malcolm and Donaldbain that Duncan is dead. Macduff simply states: *Your royal father's murdered*. He is contrasted with Macbeth at the start of Act 4, scene 3, when Malcolm wants to go and cry, but Macduff urges: *Let us rather/ Hold fast the mortal sword*. Like Macbeth, he is a man of action.

Macduff is also a passionate man. We see this in his response to Duncan's murder, and in his cry that Malcolm is not fit to live if he is really as sinful as he pretends (Act 4, scene 3). Finally, there is the heart-rending moment when Macduff hears that his family has been slaughtered. He insists that he must *feel it as a man* before he can bear it and avenge it.

Macduff has no obvious faults, but he does make one big mistake. This is leaving his family unprotected when he goes to England to seek help against Macbeth. ❍ If you have read the play, why do you think he does this?

Duncan

Duncan does not have many lines, but his role in the play is vital. As King, he is the head of the country. His murder throws the social order into chaos.

Duncan is too old to fight in battles, but he is grateful to Macbeth and Banquo for doing so. He thanks them with tears of joy in his eyes, and he rewards Macbeth. He gives Lady Macbeth a diamond to show his appreciation for her hospitality. Macbeth, in Act 1, scene 7, praises Duncan's great virtues – before stabbing him to death. If Duncan has a fault it is being too trusting.

Malcolm

Shakespeare develops Malcolm as a character more than Duncan. However, Malcolm's main importance is still as a figurehead.

It is perhaps strange that Malcolm decides to flee when Duncan's murder is discovered. This makes people suspect him and his brother, but perhaps otherwise they would have been next on the murderer's hit-list. When Malcolm returns, he has learned to be less trusting than his father. He tests Macduff's loyalty by pretending to be a sinful and destructive man. Then he admits that actually he's completely innocent.

For the play to work, we must believe that Scotland will be in safe hands after Macbeth dies, so it is more important for Malcolm to seem a reliable character than an exciting one.

The Witches

The Witches are not developed as characters in any realistic, psychological way. However, they do represent evil. They always appear on the wild moor, in equally wild weather. They talk about the spiteful acts they enjoy performing, and they lure Macbeth on to disaster. They do this not by lying, but by telling him only part of the truth.

Other characters

The most interesting minor character is Lady Macduff. She is brave and loyal, but otherwise forms a contrast to cruel Lady Macbeth. The nobles Lennox, Ross, Menteith, Angus and Caithness have little individual character. Ross is important as a messenger, as is the Captain (or 'Sergeant') who reports Macbeth's bravery.

Finally we must not forget Donaldbain – if only because it seems Shakespeare did! He is Malcolm's brother but after three short speeches in Act 2, scene 3, he disappears from the play.

Hotspot

1 Make your own character Mind Map. Compare it with the one shown here.
2 Re-read the descriptions of the characters who appear in the scene(s) that you are studying. Make a Mind Map of how their characteristics are brought out in these scenes.

Time for a scene change – take a break.

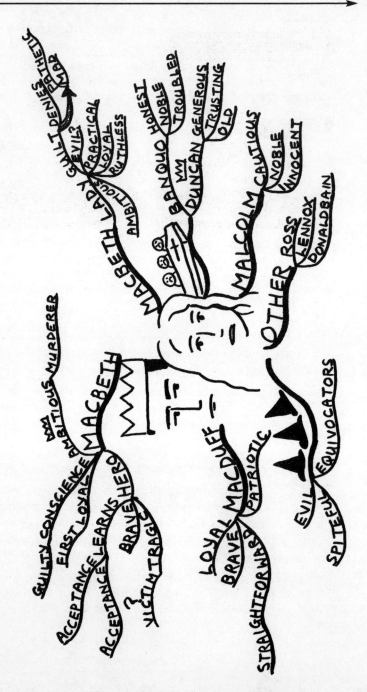

COMMENTARY

Act 1, scene 1: *The Witches set the mood*

The Witches set the story in motion. Shakespeare's audience believed in witchcraft, and in the existence of evil.

Setting: On a moor, in a storm. The place and weather help to create the right atmosphere for wild, stormy events.

SUMMARY

◆ The Witches agree to meet again, with Macbeth.

The 3rd Witch mentions Macbeth, which creates a link for us between him and them. The Witches speak to their personal spirits. These often took animal shape. *Graymalkin* is a cat, and *Paddock* a toad. *Anon* means 'At once' – so the 3rd Witch is coming straight away.

Notice the line *Fair is foul, and foul is fair*. Things have been turned upside down. The line is echoed by Macbeth's first line (Act 1, scene 3), again pointing to a link between him and the hags.

Act 1, scene 2: *Good news for some*

Setting: An army camp near Forres (north-east Scotland). A battle has been fought nearby.

SUMMARY

◆ A Captain brings news to King Duncan and his sons. Macbeth and Banquo have defeated the traitor Macdonwald and the Norwegians.
◆ Ross reports a second victory.
◆ Duncan decides to make Macbeth Thane of Cawdor.

The scene gives some **back-story** – describing events before the start of the play. Duncan's forces have been fighting a war against the Norwegians and Scottish rebels.

The wounded Captain tells of Macbeth's bravery. Macbeth is a fierce and bloody fighter. His sword *smok'd with bloody execution* – from the blood of slain enemies. He rips open Macdonwald's body, and sticks his severed head on the castle battlements.

The Thane (Lord) of Cawdor is one of the traitors. Duncan decides to give his title to Macbeth.

Act 1, scene 3: *The Witches predict*

Setting: On the moor. The storm continues. (There is thunder.)

SUMMARY

◆ The Witches discuss their evil deeds.
◆ They meet Macbeth and Banquo and predict the future for them.
◆ Ross and Angus bring the news that Macbeth is now Thane of Cawdor.
◆ Macbeth and Banquo talk about the Witches' predictions.

The captain's wife

The Witches show how spiteful they are. The 2nd Witch has been killing pigs. The 1st plans to torment a sea-captain. She will *drain him dry as hay*, prevent him from sleeping, and buffet his ship with storms. However, note that his *bark* (ship) cannot be sunk: there are limits to the Witches' powers. ❍ What might prevent them?

Here comes Macbeth!

Macbeth's first line echoes the Witches in the play's opening scene:

So foul and fair a day I have not seen.

❍ In what ways is the day both foul and fair?

The Witches greet Macbeth as *Thane of Cawdor*. We know from scene 2 that he now has this title, but as yet Macbeth does not know this. They also say he will be King. Banquo, they say, will *get* (be the father of) kings. Macbeth seems disturbed by the Witches. Banquo is less impressed, joking about their *skinny lips* and *beards*.

Ross and Angus appear and announce that Macbeth has indeed been made Thane of Cawdor. Now the first of the predictions has come true. Naturally Macbeth starts to think that the second – that he will be King – may come true as well. Banquo warns Macbeth not to believe the Witches too readily:

The instruments of darkness tell us truths;
Win us with honest trifles, to betray's
In deepest consequence.

This is exactly what the Witches do. They fool Macbeth by telling him only part of the truth. They do not lie outright.

Macbeth's thoughts are already turning to murder. Notice his **aside** (speech spoken without the other characters hearing). The idea of murdering Duncan makes his hair stand on end and his *seated heart* knock at his ribs. ❍ Is this a reasonable response to the Witches' prediction?

KEY IDEAS

One key idea is **deception**. Things may not be quite what they seem. Count how many **asides** there are. These show a character being secretive. ✪ Who speaks most of them? And as Banquo warns, evil powers may use trickery.

There is also the question of whether one can predict the future: **free will versus fate**. If the future *can* be predicted, we cannot change it by what we do. It is 'fated', so we have no free will. ✪ How far do *you* think the future is already decided?

✎ *STYLE*

The Witches' speeches are in pairs of rhymed lines, and are in a different rhythm from most of the play. Read them aloud and listen.

Act 1, scene 4: *Duncan thanks the heroes*

Setting: A room in Duncan's palace in Forres (north-east Scotland).

SUMMARY

◆ The Thane of Cawdor has been executed.
◆ Duncan thanks Macbeth and Banquo.
◆ Duncan names Malcolm as his heir.

Malcolm generously praises the courage with which the Thane of Cawdor died. Duncan reveals his own character when he admits that he gave the Thane his *absolute trust*. Note, though, Duncan's comment that one cannot *find the mind's construction in the face*: a dishonest man may look honest. ✪ Who else should Duncan be wary of?

Duncan thanks Macbeth and Banquo, getting quite emotional about it. Note that he says Banquo has *no less deserved*, yet it is Macbeth whom he rewards – perhaps because he is related to Macbeth. ✪ What do you think of this?

Duncan names Malcolm *Prince of Cumberland* – heir to the throne (just as the Prince of Wales is heir to the English throne nowadays).

Act 1, scene 5: *Lady Macbeth gets tough*

This is our first glimpse of Lady Macbeth. Think of how Shakespeare's audience would see her. In one way she is an ideal wife – loyally helping her husband. Yet women were meant to be meek, mild and motherly – not call on evil spirits to turn them into men and fill them with cruelty!

Setting: A room in Macbeth's castle in Inverness, Scotland.

SUMMARY

◆ Lady Macbeth reads about Macbeth's victory, and about the Witches.
◆ A messenger announces that Duncan will visit.
◆ Lady Macbeth plans to murder Duncan.
◆ Macbeth comes home.

A word from Will

I was rather pleased with the letter. It reminds the audience of the story so far, shows Lady Macbeth's private reaction, and shows that Macbeth confides in her. Oh – and in my day it meant the boy actor playing the part didn't have to learn that bit!

Lady Macbeth reads Macbeth's letter. It does not suggest murder – nor did the Witches, but she immediately thinks it is necessary. She does not consider waiting for the prediction to come true. Her only worry is that Macbeth may be *too full o' the milk of human kindness/ To catch the nearest way*. That is, he may be too kind to take the quickest route to the throne – murder.

Lady Macbeth's **soliloquy** (speech spoken alone), *The raven himself is hoarse …,* is powerful. Read it aloud, fiercely. She calls on evil spirits to *unsex* her – take away her womanliness, to fill her with *direst cruelty,* and to thicken her blood so that feelings of conscience cannot reach her heart.

❂ What do you think of her appeal?

Macbeth enters. He has not seen his wife for some time, but their talk is immediately of Duncan's visit. Lady Macbeth seems to take control. In answer, Macbeth says only, *We will speak further.*

✒ STYLE

Lady Macbeth calls on *thick night* to shroud herself (as in a funeral 'shroud') in the darkest smoke of hell, so that her sharp knife will not see the wound it makes (in Duncan), *Nor heaven peep through the blanket of the dark* to prevent the crime. The play is full of images of night and darkness. Here there is the special image of the stars as heavenly light peeping through holes in a blanket.

The idea of hiding things is also found in Lady Macbeth's advice to Macbeth:

> *… look like th'innocent flower/ But be the serpent under't.*

(Answers on p. 63)

1 Choose the right word: Lady Macbeth fears Macbeth's *temper / kindness / ambition.*
   She calls on *the raven / Banquo / spirits* to fill her with *cruelty / secrecy / blood.* She pictures heaven peeping through a *door / window / blanket.* She tells Macbeth to be like a *lion / bat / snake* hiding under a *blanket / flower / book.*
2 Draw this last image in your notes to help you remember it.
3 Rewrite Macbeth's letter in your own words.

Show yourself some of the milk of human kindness — take a break.

Act 1, scene 6: *Duncan comes to Inverness*

King Duncan honours the Macbeths by visiting their castle. However, he does not know that his hosts are plotting against him.

Setting: Outside Macbeth's castle.

SUMMARY

◆ King Duncan and his followers arrive at Macbeth's castle.
◆ Duncan and Banquo discuss how healthy it seems there.
◆ Lady Macbeth greets them. She seems very welcoming.

The scene begins with a flourish of music and torches. Imagine the joyful mood as the King's party arrives.

Duncan is pleased to be there. He says what a good place it is for a castle, and how sweet and fresh the air is. Banquo adds to this by observing the house martins (*the temple-haunting martlet*) that have chosen Macbeth's castle as their nesting site. He comments that where they nest, the air is healthy.

Lady Macbeth is almost too welcoming to Duncan. She says that her and Macbeth's service to him would be *poor*, even if it were *twice done, and then done double* – so great is the honour of Duncan coming to their castle.

Duncan asks, *Where's the Thane of Cawdor?* (He means Macbeth.) Good question! ✪ Where do *you* think he is? And how convincing do you find Lady Macbeth's welcome?

STYLE

Note the **dramatic irony**. As readers, or audience, we know that the Macbeths plan to murder Duncan. Yet here he is relaxed, and enjoying the fresh air and the house martins. Banquo even says what a healthy place they've come to!

Notice how Lady Macbeth makes a rhyme of Duncan's line *And thank us for your trouble* with her *... and then done double*. She is creating a sense of harmony between them.

Note: there is a 'Hotspot' for scenes 6–7 at the end of scene 7.

Act 1, scene 7: *To kill or not to kill?*

Macbeth is desperately trying to decide whether to go ahead with the plan to kill Duncan.

A word from Will

My audience believed in the Divine Right of Kings: that rulers were chosen by God. They also believed in hospitality and the strength of family ties – which made Macbeth's murder of Duncan (a guest and relative) much worse.

Setting: A room in Macbeth's castle. Elsewhere in the castle Duncan is beginning to wonder where his host is.

SUMMARY

◆ Macbeth talks himself out of murdering Duncan.
◆ He tells Lady Macbeth what he's decided.
◆ She calls him a coward.
◆ He changes his mind again.

Again, we have music and torches, reminding us of the important occasion of Duncan's visit. However, Macbeth is not giving orders, or chatting to Duncan. Instead he is alone, trying desperately to make up his mind. To kill or not to kill Duncan? ✪ How do you think he would look and act as we first see him?

Should I or shouldn't I?

Try to follow Macbeth's arguments in this speech – a soliloquy.

Macbeth's problem seems to be that he can't predict the outcome of the murder. He tells himself that if it could be over and done with, without complications, it would be better to do it quickly. He expands on this idea:

> *If th' assassination*
> *Could trammel up the consequence, and catch*
> *With his surcease, success ...*

He means that if the murder could prevent (*trammel up* = entangle) the *consequences* (such as his being found out and having to pay for his crime), he would ignore the risk of going to hell in the afterlife:

We'd jump the life to come.

Five good reasons not to kill King Duncan

Up to line 12, Macbeth is just worrying about being found out. Now he starts to think about moral reasons for not killing the King. Try to find them in the speech:

◆ They are related.
◆ He is Duncan's subject (and therefore owes him loyalty).
◆ He is Duncan's host – and should protect him, not murder him.
◆ Duncan is so good a man (*meek … virtues …*), that his death would be a great sorrow.
◆ Ambition (*Vaulting ambition* – think of a pole-vaulter!) could be Macbeth's downfall.

Lady Macbeth does her best

Lady Macbeth enters. She and her husband exchange short questions, suggesting their tense uncertainty. She worries that Duncan will find Macbeth's absence suspicious.

Macbeth announces that the murder will not go ahead: *We will proceed no further in this business.* He sounds sure – but notice that he does not mention the reasons he has just been talking about in his soliloquy. Instead he says he just wants to enjoy his new honours.

Lady Macbeth responds fiercely. She calls him a coward (*green and pale*) and accuses him of not loving her: *Such I account thy love.* She goads him about being prepared to *live a coward.* ✪ How far do you think her accusations are justified? How would you reply if you were Macbeth?

Man or beast?

Macbeth begs her to be quiet, and insists that he is brave

enough to do whatever a man should do. When he says, *Who dares do more is none*, he means that anyone who does more – such as committing murder – is an animal, not a man. This is why his wife responds with, *What beast was't then ...*

A word from Will

I wanted Lady Macbeth to frighten my audience. People in my time had fixed ideas of women as good wives and mothers. Here is a woman saying that she would dash her baby's brains out if she had sworn to do it!

Macbeth is impressed by his wife's fierceness. When he says, *If we should fail ...*, he is almost persuaded. Lady Macbeth pursues her advantage. She insists that they will not fail, then launches into her plan. They will get Duncan's attendants drunk and blame them for the murder.

The scene ends with Macbeth *settled* – resigning himself to the dire deed, and to putting on a *False face* to fool everyone.

🔑 KEY IDEAS

Macbeth's soliloquy moves from simple anxiety about being caught, to moral doubts. He struggles with his **conscience**. How should we behave? Selfishly, or morally? ✪ What would Lady Macbeth's answer be?

Another key idea is **'What is human?'** Are we animals, or does being human make us better or worse than that? ✪ What do you think?

✒ STYLE

Look again at the uncertain, thoughtful tone and gentle imagery (word pictures) of Macbeth's soliloquy – especially early on, before he starts to list his arguments. He sees life as a *bank and shoal of time* – a sandbank or shallow pool in the great sea of eternity.

Another image appears when he says that he wants to 'wear' his *Golden opinions … in their newest gloss.* Lady Macbeth uses this in her response. Clothing imagery often appears in the play. It suggests that 'appearances' may be far from the truth.

Hotspot

(Answers on p. 63)

1 (a) Why is it odd that Macbeth is alone?
  (b) What does 'We'd jump the life to come' mean?
  (c) What is the last reason Macbeth gives for not killing Duncan?
  (d) What mood is shown by the couple's short questions and answers?
  (e) With what insult does Lady Macbeth taunt Macbeth?

2 '*Untrammel*' these keywords for Macbeth's reasons for not killing Duncan:

   jectbus   teldare   shot   bitmanio   dogo

3 Complete Lady Macbeth's speech bubbles to show simply how she persuades Macbeth:

4 Use a Mind Map or chart to compare Macbeth and Lady Macbeth in scenes 6–7. Add quotes as evidence.

Hint: Consider their morality, courage, ability to deceive, and strength of character.

Don't work for an eternity — take a break!

Act 2, scene 1: *Nice night for a murder*

Try to assess the moods of the characters. The opening sets the tense mood. It also shows us more about Banquo and his relationship with Macbeth, and gives us a glimpse of Fleance. The second part shows Macbeth wound up to fever pitch. In the previous scene he itemized the reasons for not killing Duncan – but now he's going to do it anyway.

Setting: The courtyard of Macbeth's castle, past midnight.

SUMMARY

◆ Banquo, his son Fleance and a servant encounter Macbeth.
◆ Macbeth, now alone, considers the murder he is going to commit. A vision of a dagger leads him on.

An *uneasy meeting*

The moon has set, so Banquo knows it must be past midnight. The 'candles' of heaven are snuffed out too – meaning there are no stars. Picture how dark it must be. Notice Banquo's weak joke: 'There's husbandry in heaven.' He means that heaven is economizing on candles (stars). ✪ Why do you think he jokes?

Banquo's need for sleep weighs on him *like lead*, but he does not want to go to bed because he fears *cursed thoughts*. ✪ What do you think is making him anxious? Macbeth enters, but Banquo cannot see who it is, so he takes his sword back from Fleance and challenges the figure emerging from the darkness (*Who's there?*). ✪ What does this show about his mood?

26

Banquo is surprised that Macbeth is still up, but we know why he is: he plans to murder Duncan. Meanwhile the unsuspecting king has been having *unusual pleasure*. He has even given Banquo a diamond to give to Lady Macbeth, and has now gone to bed a happy man, *In measureless content*.

Banquo tells Macbeth that he has dreamed of the Witches (*the three weird sisters*). This must be one reason for Banquo's unease. He and Macbeth agree that they will talk another time. Notice how they speak to each other:

MACBETH : *… If you would grant the time.*
BANQUO: *At your kind'st leisure.*

They are old battle comrades yet they speak with polite formality. ✪ What do you think this shows about how their relationship has changed?

Banquo tells Macbeth that he will do what Macbeth wants if he can do so and yet keep his *bosom franchised* and his *allegiance clear* (his heart guilt-free, and his loyalty to Duncan clear).

The floating dagger speech

The speech falls into four parts:

1 Macbeth sees (or thinks he sees) a dagger floating in mid-air, though he realizes that it may be an illusion. It seems to beckon him towards Duncan's chamber. He notices drops (*gouts*) of blood on its blade and hilt (*dudgeon*).
2 He 'pulls himself together', telling himself *There's no such thing*. He decides that thinking about the murder (*the bloody business*) is making him see things.
3 From *Now o'er the one half-world …* he starts to think dark, fearful thoughts about the murder. He **personifies** it – picturing it as a person moving *towards his design* (his goal). He worries that the cobblestones will give him away.
4 He tells himself that he must stop talking and get on with it. Hearing a bell (probably marking 1 a.m.), he goes to kill Duncan.

A word from Will

When you read Macbeth's soliloquy, try to get a sense of his mood. A good clue is the kind of **images** (word pictures) he uses. These show how his imagination is working.

🔑 KEY IDEAS

Macbeth is at his best when he can be a **'man of action'**. That is why he tells himself to stop talking. When he starts to think about morality, he ties himself in knots.

This scene also contains the idea of **'nature'**: *Nature seems dead*. This meant at least two things to Shakespeare and his audience:

1 The natural world – the birds and animals of daylight are asleep.
2 Human nature, including Macbeth's own better nature, which previously made him decide not to kill Duncan. The murder he is about to commit is 'unnatural'.

🖊 STYLE

Follow the picture that Macbeth creates. Because it is night, *Nature seems dead* – a frightening thought. Nightmares deceive the sleeper. (Note that *curtain'd* refers to the curtains on a four-poster bed.) Witches worship their goddess, Hecate (who appears elsewhere in the play). Murder is woken (*Alarumed*) by his guard (*sentinel*) the howling wolf. He moves as quietly as a ghost, yet with big strides like those of Tarquin, an Ancient Roman villain who raped a virgin – Lucrece. (Shakespeare wrote a poem about this story.)

❂ What is the overall effect of the picture created by Macbeth?

Hotspot

(Answers on p. 63)

1 Who says each of the following lines, and what does it tell us?
   (a) *Restrain in me the cursed thoughts that/ Nature gives way to in repose.*
   (b) *Give me a sword./ Who's there?*
   (c) *... art thou but/ A dagger of the mind ...?*
   (d) *Words to the heat of deeds too cold breath gives.*

2 What is wrong in Banquo's diary entry below? Write a more accurate one.

Met Macbeth outside the castle around 11 p.m. Saw him approach in the moonlight. He seemed relaxed, and his eyes twinkled like the stars that shone overhead. He asked for my help with something, and I said, 'No problem!'

3 What part is played in Macbeth's soliloquy by each of the images (word pictures) shown below? (Re-read the speech for the answers.)

4 Mind Map Macbeth's thoughts and mood in this scene.

Take a break before you start seeing things!

Act 2, scene 2: *Partners in crime*

This scene brings out differences in the characters of Macbeth and Lady Macbeth. As with Act 1, scene 7, Lady Macbeth's behaviour would seem particularly unladylike to Shakespeare's audience. Women were *not* supposed to go around carrying bloody daggers!

Setting: The courtyard of Macbeth's castle, some time before dawn.

SUMMARY

◆ Macbeth joins Lady Macbeth after the murder.
◆ Macbeth is terrified of his crime, and already regrets it.
◆ Lady Macbeth attempts to calm him down.
◆ She returns the daggers to Duncan's chamber.

Bold Lady Macbeth

Lady Macbeth enters alone. The wine that made Duncan's attendants drunk has given her courage. She has drugged the attendants so heavily that it is uncertain whether they will live. Hearing Macbeth, she worries that he may not yet have murdered Duncan:

> *Alack, I am afraid they have awaked,*
> *And 'tis not done; th'attempt and not the deed*
> *Confounds us.*

She means that if they bungle the murder they will be ruined.

Notice her comment, *Had he not resembled/ My father as he slept, I had done't.* She is saying that she would have murdered Duncan had he not looked like her own father.
✪ Compare this with her bold claim in Act 1, scene 7.

(She says she would dash her own baby's brains out if she had to.) How tough is she really?

I *have done the deed*

The conversation begins in short, jerky sentences, showing the tension. Lady Macbeth speaks again of hearing the *owl scream* (a sign of bad luck). Macbeth now regrets the murder. To him his bloody hands are *a sorry sight*. Lady Macbeth tells him he's a fool to say that. He describes how when Macbeth and Donaldbain said their prayers he could not say *Amen*, as a Christian should. ✪ Why should this worry him?

Notice that while Macbeth is almost mad with guilt and fear, his wife's approach is down-to-earth. She will not let her imagination get the better of her. She tells him:

> *Consider it not so deeply.*
> *   … These deeds must not be thought*
> *After these ways; so, it will make us mad.*

She means: 'Don't think about it so much. We musn't think about the murder like this or we'll go mad.' This hints at what eventualy happens: she does go mad. Macbeth seems close to madness now, but later he becomes very clear-headed. ✪ Which approach, then, is more effective in the long run?

Macbeth lets imagination get the better of him. He says he has murdered sleep *that knits up the ravelled sleeve of care* – healing the sleeper's worried mind like someone repairing a shirt sleeve. This poetic language is inappropriate when action is needed. Lady Macbeth has no idea what he means. She tells him off for bringing the daggers from the chamber.

She reminds him that the attendants must be smeared with blood, and the daggers left to make them seem guilty. Macbeth cannot make himself go back in, so Lady Macbeth calls him a coward and returns the daggers herself. When she gets back, she again calls her husband a coward (*To wear a heart so white*).

As the scene closes, we hear determined knocking at the castle gate.

A word from Will

I wanted the audience to ask 'Who's that knocking? Will the Macbeths be found out now?' Think of the effect on stage. Unknown people are arriving, and the exhausted couple must get ready to act innocent when Duncan is found dead. The knocking also hints at the siege of Macbeth castle in Act 5.

⚷ KEY IDEAS

Compare how Macbeth and his wife view their crime. (See 'Style', below.) Throughout the rest of the play, Macbeth is gradually coming to terms with his **conscience**, accepting what he has done. Lady Macbeth, meanwhile, gradually falls apart.

STYLE

Water is an important image in this scene. It shows how differently Macbeth and his wife think. She tells him:

> *Go get some water*
> *And wash this filthy witness from your hand.*

Near the end of the scene she says:

> *A little water clears us of this deed.*
> *How easy is it then!*

She thinks they can 'wash their hands' of the crime. Macbeth feels that the whole ocean will not be enough to wash the blood – or the sin – from his hands. Instead, his bloody hands will make the green sea *incarnadine* (lines 60–4). Notice how Shakespeare here says the same thing twice: once for the educated people in the audience (*multitudinous seas incarnadine*), and again for the 'groundlings' (*making the green one red*).

Hotspot

(Answers on p. 63)

1 Who says each of the following lines, and what does it tell us?

(a) *That which hath made them drunk hath made me bold.*

(b) *… the attempt and not the deed/ Confounds us.*

(c) *This is a sorry sight.*

(d) *A little water clears us of this deed.*

2 Imagine Duncan is now a ghost. How would he describe his last night alive?

3 Imagine the Macbeths decide to confess. Write their statements to the police describing events on the night of the murder. Remember that each might see things differently.

Have you made multitudinous Mind Maps?
Take a break!

Act 2, scene 3: *O horror! horror! horror!*

The scene begins with some **comic relief** – the drunken Porter. This gives the audience a break after several tense scenes before the drama of Macduff discovering the body.

Setting: As in the previous scene, the courtyard of Macbeth's castle in Inverness, just inside the locked gate.

SUMMARY

◆ The Porter jokes about the knocking, then opens up.

◆ Strange events are reported.

◆ Macduff finds Duncan dead.

◆ Malcolm and Donaldbain decide to flee.

The porter at the gates of Hell

The scene starts with the same knocking which frightened Macbeth as the end of scene 2. On stage there hardly needs to be a scene change – just a moment when the stage is empty.

The Porter has been drinking until after dawn. He is either still drunk now, or has a bad hangover. Either would explain his slowness in opening the gate.

This is rather dark 'comic relief'. The Porter jokes about who might be knocking. He imagines himself as the Porter of Hell, asking *Who's there I'th'name of Beelzebub* – a chief devil (pronounced *Be-elzee-bub*). He runs through a list of evil-doers who might be at the gate. There is **dramatic irony** in the image of Macbeth's castle as Hell. The audience knows this is more accurate than the Porter realizes.

Macduff shows himself to be a good-humoured man. He is prepared to joke with the Porter, even after being kept waiting, and to listen to the Porter's comments on the effects of alcohol.

Strange goings-on

While Macduff goes to wake Duncan, Lennox tells Macbeth about strange events in the night – stormy weather, *strange screams of death*, the owl clamouring all night, and the earth shaking. ✪ Why do you suppose Macbeth's answer is so brief?

Murder most horrid

Macduff returns with terrible news. At first all he can say is *O horror! horror! horror!* He cannot spell out what has happened. He sees confusion, or chaos, as to blame, and then speaks of murder breaking open the *temple* – Duncan's body. The *Gorgon* he mentions refers to the Gorgons in Greek myth. Anyone who looked at them was turned to stone.

A word from Will

In my day people saw kings as being chosen by God. When a king was crowned his head was *anointed* with holy oil.

The interest for the audience now is 'How will everyone react?' Macduff refuses to tell Lady Macbeth the news because he thinks it would kill a woman. This is **ironic** when we think about what Lady Macbeth is really like. When she hears the news her response is: *What, in our house?* Banquo notices the oddness of this straight away.

Macbeth's speech, *Had I but died an hour before this chance*, sounds sincere. He genuinely regrets the murder. He sounds less convincing after this, and Lady Macbeth's fainting fit is probably to distract everyone from her husband. ✪ Does it work?

Malcolm and Donaldbain flee. ✪ What impression do you think this is likely to make?

🔑 *KEY IDEAS*

In Shakespeare's plays when things are seriously wrong in the kingdom, this is reflected in **nature**. The screaming sounds, the clamouring owl and the moving earth are all bad signs.

🖊 *STYLE*

The Porter speaks in **prose** – not in **verse** (poetry), because he is a lowly character, not a noble.

Macbeth sounds insincere when he tells Malcolm and Donaldbain the news. Compare his flowery line *… the fountain of your blood/ Is stopped* with honest Macduff's simple *Your royal father's murdered.*

Macduff finds Macbeth's killing of Duncan's attendants suspicious. And Macbeth's words are too poetic to be convincing. It is as if he is trying too hard to seem grief-stricken. See, especially, *His silver skin laced with his golden blood.* (He sounds colour-blind!)

Hotspot

(Answers on pp. 63–4)

1 Who says each of the following lines, and what does it tell us?
 (a) *What three things does drink especially provoke?*
 (b) *'Twas a rough night.*
 (c) *Ring the alarum bell.*
 (d) *What, in our house?*

2 Whose private thoughts might these be?
 (a) Now we won't be able to question them. Suspicious!
 (b) Must seem really grief-stricken!
 (c) They'll suspect him. I must do something!
 (d) Now they'll suspect my younger brother and me.

3 Make a Mind Map (and/or mark your copy of the play) to show how the mood changes during this scene, and how actors could show it.

Time you had some comic relief!

Act 2, scene 4: *Ill omens*

Setting: Outside Macbeth's castle.

SUMMARY

◆ An Old Man and Ross discuss strange events.
◆ Macduff joins them and says he will not be attending Macbeth's coronation.

Little actually happens in this scene, but it is important, all the same. Ross and the Old Man discuss the *unnatural* events – signs in nature that things are badly wrong in Scotland. Macduff enters with the news that Malcolm and Donaldbain (Duncan's sons) have fled. As he says, this makes them look guilty of the murder. ✪ Do you think they were wise to flee?

Duncan's body has been carried to *Colmekill* – Iona, where Scottish kings were buried. Macbeth has gone to Scone to be crowned. Significantly, Macduff says he will not be attending, though Ross will. ✪ Why do you think Macduff chooses not to?

Act 3, scene 1: *Invitation to a feast*

Macbeth tries to make his position secure.

Setting: A room in the palace at Forres – which now belongs to Macbeth.

SUMMARY

◆ Banquo thinks about the Witches.
◆ Macbeth invites Banquo to the feast.
◆ Macbeth persuades himself that Banquo must die.
◆ Macbeth gets two men to kill Banquo.

The invitation

Macbeth plans to remove the first threat to his position – Banquo. In doing so he begins to act independently of his wife. The scene begins with a short **soliloquy** (solo speech) from Banquo which suggests that Macbeth is right to see him as a threat. Banquo fears that Macbeth *playe'dst most foully* for his crown. At the same time he hopes to benefit from the Witches' prophecies himself.

Macbeth invites Banquo to the feast which will celebrate the fact that Macbeth is now King. Yet he is planning to have Banquo and his son murdered. Macbeth's words *Fail not our feast* (Don't miss it) are **ironic**. Banquo does not 'fail' the feast, but he does rather spoil it! (See Act 3, scene 4.)

The justification

Macbeth speaks an important **soliloquy**, beginning *To be thus is nothing*. He means that being King is no good unless he can make his position safe.

Macbeth fears Banquo's *royalty of nature … dauntless temper* and *wisdom*. Moreover, Macbeth feels somehow made small or timid by Banquo. He also hates the idea that he has

murdered Duncan and *filed* (defiled, dirtied) his mind just for
Banquo's descendants to reap the benefits.

Winding up the murderers

Macbeth persuades two men that they have good reason to
want Banquo dead, and that if they are real men, they will get
revenge by killing him.

 STYLE

See how Macbeth taunts the men to make them agree to his
plan – rather as Lady Macbeth taunted him earlier. He
compares different types of dog with different types of man.
He suggests that they may just be *mongrels*, but that if they are
not i'th'worst rank of manhood then they will kill Banquo.

Act 3, scene 2: *Macbeth – a worried man*

This scene shows the relationship between Macbeth and his
wife changing.

Setting: Another room in the royal palace.

SUMMARY

◆ Macbeth is anxious.
◆ Lady Macbeth tries to calm him down.
◆ Macbeth hints at the coming murder.

We have scorched the snake, not killed it

Lady Macbeth expresses her worries to Macbeth. He is
spending time on his own, thinking the *sorriest fancies* about
the dead Duncan. She urges him to put an end to this:

> *Things without all remedy*
> *Should be without regard.*

She means, in effect, 'No use crying over spilled milk' – or
spilled blood! ❖ What do you think of her advice?

Macbeth says that they have not yet killed *the snake* – that is, their ambitions are only half-fulfilled, because they are not yet safe. He also speaks of the *terrible dreams/ That shake us nightly.* If you have read the scene following Duncan's murder you may remember the voice saying *Macbeth hath murdered sleep.* This sleeplessness – a sign of a guilty conscience – continues to afflict Macbeth and his wife.

Macbeth seems to envy Duncan, who is dead but at peace.

Gentle my lord

Lady Macbeth is worried that Macbeth's *rugged looks* will make their guests suspicious. He must be *bright and jovial.* You may remember how, earlier in the play, she told him to be like a snake hiding beneath an innocent flower. Here again she urges him to pretend. Macbeth speaks bitterly. She tells him simply, *You must leave this,* worried that he is driving himself mad. Macbeth admits his mind is *full of scorpions.*

The hint

Macbeth drops a hint that he is getting rid of Banquo and Fleance – another *deed of dreadful note.* Yet when she asks what the deed is, he replies: *Be innocent of the knowledge, dearest chuck.* Memorize this line! It shows that Macbeth is now acting independently of his wife. See how she reacts at the end of the scene. This is not the man she knows.

KEY IDEAS

Note the familiar idea of **disguise and deception**. The line *… make our faces vizards to our hearts* sums this up. There is also the idea of human nature compared with animal nature (see 'Style', below).

STYLE

Notice the animal imagery – a snake (again!), scorpions, a bat, a beetle and a crow. They are all dangerous, or dark, or night animals. They also suggest that Macbeth is becoming more like a beast, and less human.

Macbeth's closing speech is darkly beautiful. It also shows that he is welcoming his fate, inviting the night to fall. Look at the **imagery** (word pictures). He asks night to *scarf up* (bandage) the *tender eye of pitiful day* (the sun), and to tear up the *bond* (a legal document) that is Banquo's life. Macbeth describes night falling, as if it is his own special time. He has become a creature of the darkness – one of the *black agents*.

Act 3, scene 3: *One down, one to go*

Setting: A road running through the palace park.

SUMMARY

◆ The two murderers are joined by a third.
◆ They kill Banquo but Fleance escapes.

Macbeth is so distrustful now that he has sent a third man to make sure the other two keep to the plan. There is confusion. One man strikes out the torchlight, and in the darkness Fleance gets away.

Act 3, scene 4: *Banquo puts in a late appearance*

Think about how you would direct this powerful scene – especially how you would handle Banquo's ghost. Is it real and only visible to Macbeth, or does he imagine it?

A word from Will

My audience believed in ghosts. (Do you?) Of course they could see Banquo's ghost onstage – large as life. Still, some of the clever ones wondered if the ghost was really just in Macbeth's mind. After all, no one else sees it.

Setting: The palace banqueting hall. Picture a long table spread with food and drink. The highest-ranking people would sit near Macbeth and his wife.

SUMMARY

◆ Macbeth and Lady Macbeth welcome the guests.
◆ One of the murderers enters. He says Banquo is dead but Fleance has escaped.
◆ Banquo's ghost appears (twice) and terrifies Macbeth.
◆ Lady Macbeth tries to smooth things over, then gives up and asks everyone to go.

Your humble host

Macbeth and his wife are doing their best to be good hosts. Macbeth makes a special effort to *mingle with society and play the humble host.*

At this point one of the three murderers from scene 3 comes in and gives Macbeth 'some good news and some bad news'. The good is that Banquo is dead, the bad that Fleance escaped. So now the Witches' prophecy may come true: Fleance could grow up to be King.

Macbeth is distracted by this. He refers to Banquo as a *serpent* and Fleance as a *worm* (a baby serpent). His wife – *Sweet remembrancer* – makes him remember his job as host.

Who's that sitting in **my** chair?

A worse distraction now appears (but only to Macbeth!). Remember that Macbeth is still on his feet. When he looks for his place, he thinks the table is full. Then he realizes that there's a ghost sitting in his seat.

Macbeth loses control, blaming the guests as if they put the ghost there, and denies the murder. Lady Macbeth tries to take control, telling the guests to ignore her raving husband and enjoy their food. Then she turns to her husband, and tells him his fear is making him imagine things again. As ever, she is down-to-earth: *You look but on a stool.*

In his *Blood hath been shed ...* speech Macbeth says more than enough to make the guests suspect him. He is basically saying that in the good old days when you murdered someone they stayed dead – but not anymore!

Once again Lady Macbeth brings her husband round: *Your noble friends do lack you*. And once again he makes an effort to pretend. He even leads a toast *to our dear friend Banquo, whom we miss;/ Would he were here!* He changes his tune when Banquo's ghost reappears – as if invited. Lady Macbeth once again tries to persuade everyone that Macbeth's behaviour is normal.

Read Macbeth's speech beginning *What man dare, I dare*.
○ What seems to you to be his main concern here? What does he want to prove?

Stand not upon the order of your going

Lady Macbeth finally gives up on the banquet. She hurries the guests out, urging them not to worry about leaving in rank order. This reflects how everything in the world of the play is becoming disordered.

With the guests gone, Macbeth reflects gloomily on how *blood will have blood* – murder will be revenged. It is now almost dawn. Macbeth asks his wife what she makes of Macduff not coming to the feast, and comments on how he now keeps a spy in every household. Lady Macbeth, sensible as ever, tells Macbeth that his main problem is lack of sleep. ○ Is she right?

 KEY IDEAS

Macbeth's speech beginning *What man dare, I dare* touches on his worries about proving his **manhood**. He does not want to seem to be *the baby of a girl*. He says he can handle bears and tigers but not ghosts. He is at his best when he knows what he's fighting.

✑ **STYLE**

The scene is full of dramatic variety. Macbeth is sane one moment and raving the next, and his wife switches rapidly between trying to calm him down and pretending to her guests that everything is all right. Then there's the small matter of a real or imaginary ghost popping in and out!

Hotspot

(Answers on p. 64)

1 Quiz time:
   (a) Who is called a worm?
   (b) Who's stool does the ghost sit on?
   (c) What else has Macbeth previously imagined?
   (d) What does Macbeth keep in every household?
   (e) What does Lady Macbeth think Macbeth needs?
2 With a friend, roleplay a discussion between Macbeth and his psychotherapist (or psychiatrist). How would Macbeth describe his 'ghostly' experiences? What questions would a therapist ask? What advice would he/she give (if any)?
3 Mind Map, then write, Lady Macbeth's letter about the scene to a magazine problem page.

Macbeth needs a break, and so do you.

Act 3, scene 5: *Hecate's not happy*

Setting: The moor in a storm.

SUMMARY

◆ Hecate meets the Witches.

Hecate, goddess of witchcraft tells the Witches off for 'trading and trafficking' with Macbeth without her. She also complains that he is only interested in personal gain, and she plans to trick him.

A word from Will

Sorry about this scene! Audiences wanted more of the Witches, so the theatre got someone else to add this bit. I hate to say it, but his style's not as good as mine, is it?

Act 3, scene 6: *Believe that and you'll believe anything*

Setting: A room in the royal palace at Forres, Scotland.

SUMMARY

◆ Lennox and another lord meet and discuss recent events.
◆ Malcolm is with the English king. Macduff has gone there to ask for help.

This is another scene in which nothing actually happens. Nevertheless it is important because of what it tells us. Lennox speaks **ironically**. He does not actually believe what he is saying. Rather, he is presenting the 'official' version of events as if he did believe it.

We hear from the lord that Malcolm has found refuge with King Edward. Macduff has gone to appeal to Edward for help against Macbeth.

Act 4, scene 1: *What's cooking?*

For Shakespeare's audience, witches were no joke. Most people believed that they really were evil, and could cast spells and foretell the future. Women were still hanged as witches – or in some countries burnt at the stake. The goddess of witchcraft, taken from Ancient Greek myths, was Hecate (pronounced He-*car*-te.)

A word from Will

I wanted to flatter King James when I wrote this play – a royal performance is always good publicity! So, I twisted history to favour his ancestor Banquo. (The real Macbeth was quite a good king!) The 'procession' of kings represents James's ancestors. And of course I knew he was keen on witchcraft – he wrote a book about it.

Setting: A cave on the moor. To Shakespeare's audience a moor would seem wild and dangerous – not a nice picnic spot. The cave would be even more dangerous, lit only by torchlight, and perhaps leading to hell itself!

SUMMARY

◆ The Witches speak to their spirit 'familiars'.
◆ They stir ingredients into the cauldron.
◆ They show Macbeth three visions.
◆ They reveal the future – a long line of kings descended from Banquo.
◆ Macbeth decides to murder Macduff's family.

The brew

The Witches speak to their spirit familiars (personal spirits). Then they throw their foul ingredients into the cauldron to make their spell for Macbeth. The ingredients were all thought to be poisonous, or at least pretty nasty. Most come from animals, which reflects a key idea in the play – people sometimes behave like savage beasts.

The Witches chant as they add the ingredients. Chanting has an effect on the body, mind and emotions. That's why it's used on the football terraces! (See under 'Style' below for more.)

Hecate, goddess of witchcraft (or waste of space!)

Hecate enters and congratulates the Witches. It is unlikely that Shakespeare wrote these lines, because they are a little dull, as is Hecate's other speech. The speeches were probably added in response to popular demand for more of the Witches. Hecate has nothing else to do in the scene.

Macbeth demands to be told

Macbeth enters and immediately demands answers to his questions. He does not care how much harm it causes. His *I conjure you ...* speech (line 50 onwards) presents images of awful destruction. In response the hags show him three apparitions, of their spirit masters.

Remember they are powerful evil spirits – even those that appear as children! Picture them:

1 **Armoured head**. Could suggest war, or Macbeth's own head cut off in Act 5. It warns Macbeth, *beware Macduff*. Macbeth is eventually killed and beheaded by Macduff.
2 **Bloody child**. Tells Macbeth to be savage, bold and determined Macbeth, and that he need not fear any man *of woman born*. Macbeth is comforted. He does not know that Macduff was cut out of his mother's womb, so is not quite 'of woman born'.
3 **Crowned child carrying a tree**. This spirit tells Macbeth that he will not be beaten so long as Birnam Wood does not come to Dunsinane Hill (site of Macbeth's castle). They are 12 miles apart, and woods don't walk, so Macbeth feels safe! But in the end Malcolm's soldiers hack down branches from the wood as camouflage, so the wood *does* come to Dunsinane.

✪ How safe should Macbeth feel?

Will Banquo's descendants be kings?

Macbeth now wants to know, *shall Banquo's issue ever/ Reign in this kingdom?* (Banquo's son Fleance got away when Banquo was murdered on Macbeth's orders.) The Witches say, *Seek to know no more.* (In modern terms, 'You don't want to know!') But Macbeth is determined. He threatens the Witches, so they show him a procession of kings, followed by Banquo's ghost, smiling.

Macbeth apparently has no children, though Lady Macbeth says she has *given suck* to a baby. Perhaps it died.

The kings carrying *two-fold balls* (orbs – symbols of power), refer to James ruling both Scotland and England. The *treble sceptres* also refer to James. A sceptre was a rod used in the coronation ceremony (crowning kings and queens). Scotland used one, England two.

'Er ... did you see three hags with a big cauldron?'

Lennox (one of two lords discussing Macbeth in Act 3, scene 6) has not seen the Witches. ✪ Do you think Macbeth imagined them? Lennox announces that Macduff has fled to England – so Macbeth (perhaps over-reacting?) decides to murder Macduff's family.

The visions have made Macbeth think he cannot be harmed. On the other hand, they have told him that he will have no heir. He decides that from now on he will act first and think later:

> *The very firstlings of my heart shall be*
> *The firstlings of my hand.*

 STYLE

Notice that the style of the Witches' chant differs from the **blank verse** that Shakespeare uses elsewhere. Blank verse has five pairs of **syllables** (the smallest parts of a word that you can say) in each line and does not rhyme (blank = unrhymed). Take Macbeth's line:

The **ca**stle **of** Mac**duff** I **will** sur**prise**.

Beat this out with your hand, emphasizing the syllables as shown.

✪ How many pairs of syllables (or beats) are there in a line of the Witches' chant? How does it rhyme? Ask your teacher if you're unsure of this.

🗝 *KEY IDEAS*

Two important ideas emerge in this scene:

◆ **Fate**. Shakespeare explores whether it is possible to predict events, and whether everything is 'fated' to happen. ✪ What do *you* think about this?

◆ **Kingship**. It is not enough for Macbeth to be king. He wants to start a 'dynasty', a line of kings – his son, grandson, great-grandson, and so on.

✪ What are your views on these ideas?

Hotspot

(Answers on p. 64)

1 MacCookery time! Fill in the different parts required for each ingredient for the Witches' brew from the list:

adder's ____   Jew's ____
baboon's ____   lizard's ____
baby owl's ____   newt's ____
baby's ____   shark's ____ and ____
bat's ____   slow-worm's ____
dog's ____   Tartar's ____
dragon's ____   tiger's ____
frog's ____   Turk's ____
hemlock ____   wolf's ____

Parts: eye, toe wool, tongue, tongue, sting, leg, wing, scale, tooth, stomach, throat, root, liver, nose, lips, finger, guts, blood. Check your answers in the text.

2 Mind Map, or write in your own words, what each spirit reveals to Macbeth, and how the information turns out to be accurate. Look back through this section for the answers.

3 You are Lennox. Describe to a friend how Macbeth looked coming out of the cave.

Feel a bit blank? Take a break before things get any verse!

Act 4, scene 2: *Lady Macduff and her son*

Lady Macduff and her son appear only in this short, sad scene, in 'cameo' roles. Lady Macduff is a contrast to Lady Macbeth. In her son we see his father's brave loyalty. Their murder spurs Macduff on by giving him a personal grudge against Macbeth.

Setting: Macduff castle in Fife (Scotland).

SUMMARY

◆ Ross and Lady Macduff discuss Macduff's flight.
◆ Lady Macduff discusses her husband with her son.
◆ A messenger warns of danger.
◆ Lady Macbeth and her son are murdered.

What was Macduff thinking of?

A dark shadow hangs over this scene: in scene 1 Macbeth announced his intention to have Macduff's family murdered. So we know as we listen to the touching conversation between mother and son that they are about to die.

Lady Macduff cannot understand why Macduff left his family undefended. ✪ What do you make of it? Ross does his best to reassure her:

> *Things at the worst will cease, or else climb upward*
> *To what they were before.*

He means 'Things can only get better.' He leaves, worried that if he stays he will start to cry. ✪ Should he stay?

Sirrah, your father's dead

Perhaps Lady Macduff means that Macduff may as well be dead if he's in England and they remain in Scotland. Lady Macduff affectionately yet sadly teases the boy. He gives clever answers, refusing to believe that his father is dead.

The mood becomes urgent when the anxious messenger warns of approaching danger. Lady Macduff does not panic, but comments bitterly that her innocence is no protection in this wicked world. The murderers enter and Lady Macduff shows her loyalty to her husband by insulting them. They kill the boy and pursue the mother – who has no chance of escape.
✪ How do you feel about the boy's last line?

Act 4, scene 3: *Macduff is tested*

For the play to have a satisfying ending, we need to believe that Malcolm will be a good king. Also bear in mind that Shakespeare's audience believed that kings were chosen by God.

Setting: Outside King Edward's palace, England. This is the only scene set outside Scotland.

SUMMARY

◆ Malcolm tests Macduff's loyalty.
◆ We hear of Edward's healing powers.
◆ Ross brings the news that Macduff's family are dead.

Doubts about Macduff

Malcolm distrusts Macduff at first. After all, Macduff was once loyal to Macbeth. Malcolm also wonders why Macduff felt he could leave his family unprotected. Perhaps, he thinks, it was because he had made a deal with Macbeth. There is **dramatic irony** here: we know that Macduff's family were far from safe.

We can see that Malcolm has become more careful than Duncan was. At the same time he apologizes, admitting that Macduff may be innocent.

I'm really bad

Malcolm tests Macduff by accusing himself of three sins – lust, greed and destructiveness. Macduff excuses him at first. Eventually Malcolm says he would like to *Uproar the universal peace, confound/ All unity on earth.* This is too much for Macduff, who says Malcolm is unfit to live – let alone be King. This answer reassures Malcolm that Macduff is honest, and loyal to Scotland.

Edward's healing powers

A doctor says that a crowd of sick people are hoping to be cured by King Edward. Malcolm explains to Macduff that the

King has the power to heal people of a disease called *the Evil* (scrofula). This speech emphasizes the divine power of kings (including James I), but it is often cut from performances because it is not essential to the plot.

Bad news

Ross at first cannot bring himself to reveal his most tragic piece of news. Eventually he admits that he has news that should be *howled out in the desert air*. It is of course the massacre of Macduff's family.

Macduff can hardly take it in. Malcolm urges him to *Dispute it [bear it] like a man* and to *let grief convert to anger*, spurring him to revenge. He ends the scene with a hint of hope: *The night is long that never finds the day*. In other words, no night lasts for ever. Nor can any national disaster.

⊙━━ᵣ KEY IDEAS

This scene revisits the idea of the **Divine Right of Kings** – and the perfect king. It also looks at **manhood**. Macduff is no milksop, but he is clearly grief-stricken at the news of his family. He insists that he *must feel it as a man*.

✐ STYLE

Notice the animal imagery: Malcolm calls himself an *innocent lamb*; Macduff's family are *murdered deer*; Macbeth is a *hell-kite* who has slain Macduff's *pretty chickens*.

(Answers on p. 64)

1 Of which three sins does Malcolm accuse himself? Choose from: untidiness   lust   dishonesty   cowardice   greed overspending   laziness   overeating   destructiveness
2 Match the following lines with the speaker and what the lines show us:

(a) *Angels are bright still, though the brightest fell.*
(b) *Why in that rawness left you wife and child –*
(c) *Fit to govern!/ No, not to live.*
(d) *No; they were well at peace when I did leave 'em.*
(e) *But I must also feel it as a man.*
Macduff has feelings.
Ross cannot bring himself to break the news.
Malcolm knows some men are good.
Macduff is honest, and loyal to Scotland.
Malcolm is cautious about trusting people.

3 Make a Mind Map for a director's notes. How should Ross show that he is keeping something back? How should Macduff show his feelings?

Understood why Malcolm tests Macduff? Take a break before testing yourself again.

Act 5, scene 1: *Lady Macbeth is losing her mind*

We have not seen Lady Macbeths for a while. Now she is a changed woman.

Setting: A room in Macbeth's castle in Dunsinane.

SUMMARY

◆ A doctor and a lady-in-waiting discuss Lady Macbeth's illness.
◆ Lady Macbeth walks and talks in her sleep.
◆ The doctor says he can't help her.

*S*leep-writing

The *Waiting-Gentlewoman* (companion to Lady Macbeth) tells the doctor that she has seen Lady Macbeth write a letter in her sleep. He says this is a sign of *great perturbation in nature* – Lady Macbeth is mentally disturbed. The gentlewoman has also heard Lady Macbeth say things in her sleep too terrible to repeat to the doctor.

Out, damned spot!

Lady Macbeth enters, rubbing her hands – as the gentlewoman has seen her do before. She is trying to wash off a stain that can never be removed. She talks in a confused way. ❂ What do you think the lines below refer to?

1 *... who would have thought the old man to have had so much blood in him?*
2 *The Thane of Fife had a wife. Where is she now?*

If you're unsure, look back to Act 2, scene 2, and Act 4, scene 2. In the first, Macbeth and Lady Macbeth do something dreadful; in the second, Macbeth has something dreadful done without Lady Macbeth's help.

Lady Macbeth is a broken woman. Compare this with the powerful, determined character that she was earlier. Notice her despairing line, *all the perfumes of Arabia will not sweeten this little hand. O, O, O.* ❂ How do you feel about her now?

 STYLE

Notice that now she is mad, Lady Macbeth speaks in prose. Her uneven, disjointed speech would not fit well into verse. Notice, too, the little rhyme about the Thane of Fife. ❂ With what age group would you normally associate little rhymes like this? What does this tell us about Lady Macbeth?

Act 5, scene 2: *The English army approaches*

As the pace hots up, the scenes get shorter.

Setting: Countryside not far from Macbeth's castle.

SUMMARY

◆ Scottish lords discuss their enemy, Macbeth.

Scottish lords discuss the situation. The English army, headed by Malcolm, is nearby. Both Malcolm and Macduff burn to avenge themselves on Macbeth. ☉ What for?

Some people are saying that Macbeth is mad, others that he shows *valiant fury*. Either way, the lords agree that things are looking bad for him.

Act 5, scene 3: *Doctor, doctor*

We see Macbeth, hard-pressed but still trusting in the Witches' promises of his safety.

Setting: Macbeth's castle at Dunsinane.

SUMMARY

◆ A servant tells Macbeth that the English army is in sight.
◆ Macbeth asks a doctor about Lady Macbeth.

Go, prick thy face

Macbeth is preparing for battle. He shows signs of stress. He is probably still not sleeping, he has the guilt of several murders on his conscience – and he is now surrounded by enemies. His mood swings wildly, from defiantly confident to *sick at heart*.

He thinks he is safe *Till Birnam Wood remove to Dunsinane*, and until he meets a man *not born of woman*. However, he angrily tells a young servant, pale-faced with fear, to prick his face and spread the blood over his *linen cheeks* to put some colour into them.

Throw physic to the dogs

In the second part of this short scene, Macbeth talks to Seyton (his general) and to a doctor. Although far from calm, Macbeth has become fearless and determined. He says he will fight until the flesh is hacked from his bones. His impatience makes him call for his armour before he needs it. Then he changes his mind – *Bring it after me*.

He asks if the doctor cannot cure Lady Macbeth of the *thick-coming fancies* (crowding thoughts) that trouble her. He loses patience with the doctor's inability to do this, and dismisses medicine (*physic*). Bitterly, he asks what rhubarb, senna or other laxative drug the doctor can recommend to get rid of the English army.

Act 5, scene 4: *Malcolm branches out*

Setting: Near Birnam Wood. Another rapid scene change, as the climax hurries on.

SUMMARY

◆ Macbeth's enemies approach.
◆ Malcolm tells his soldiers to cut down branches.

Malcolm's army arrives at Birnam Wood. Malcolm gets every soldier to cut down a branch and carry it before him as camouflage. He says that those who fight on Macbeth's side have been *constrained* – forced, and have no heart for it.

Act 5, scene 5: *Lady Macbeth's sad end*

A short pause in the quickening pace of the play, as Macbeth responds to his wife's death. (A 'Hotspot' for these last four scenes comes after the final scene.)

Setting: Inside Macbeth's castle.

SUMMARY

◆ Macbeth boasts that his castle will withstand a siege.
◆ Lady Macbeth dies.
◆ Birnam Wood comes to Dunsinane.

Confidence

Macbeth is confident that his castle is too strong for the enemy: they will eventually die from hunger and sickness. His boast is interrupted by a *cry of women*. For a moment we see how much Macbeth has changed. At one time he was terrified by guilt and ghosts, but now he has *almost forgot the taste of fears.*

Then the news arrives: the cry of women was for Lady Macbeth, who has died – by suicide (as we learn from Malcolm in the final scene). Macbeth's line, *She should have died hereafter,* could mean 'She would have died at some time or other anyway'; or it could mean 'She should have died later – perhaps after the battle, or simply in old age.' ❂ How do you interpret it, and why?

A *walking wood*

It is a powerful dramatic moment onstage when the messenger fearfully comes to Macbeth to announce that there is a *moving grove* – a walking wood – heading towards the castle. Now Macbeth begins to despair: *I 'gin to be aweary of the sun.* Even so, he is determined to die in armour – *with harness on our back.* ❂ How do you feel about Macbeth now?

Macbeth now gives up his idea of playing a waiting game while the enemy starve. He orders a charge out of the castle: *Arm, arm and out!*

A word from Will

I hope you admire Macbeth at least a bit. Otherwise he wouldn't be a tragic hero – and this is meant to be a tragedy! I see him as a man who's made huge mistakes – yet who is still noble at least in his brave acceptance of his fate.

🔑 KEY IDEAS

Deception is a key idea in the play, and now Macbeth realizes that he's been deceived by *the equivocation of the fiend.* Equivocation is deceiving without actually lying outright, and the fiend is the devil.

STYLE

This scene contains a beautiful but pessimistic speech –
Macbeth's reaction to his wife's death. Read it – preferably
aloud – and imagine the thoughts and images in Macbeth's
head. He pictures the future days creeping meaninglessly in a
petty pace. They stretch ahead – suggested by the repeated
Tomorrow until the end of time.

The past has been equally pointless and meaningless – only
lighting fools *The way to dusty death*. (Notice the **alliteration** –
the depressed-sounding repetition of the 'd' sound.) The *brief
candle* is a **metaphor** for life. That is, Macbeth refers to life as
a candle, because both soon die, losing their light and heat.
❍ What other metaphors does Macbeth use for life in this
speech?

Act 5, scene 6: *Branches down, lads*

Setting: A plain before Macbeth's castle.

SUMMARY

◆ Malcolm's army gets ready.

This is the shortest scene in the play. The pace is hotting up
again. Malcolm tells the soldiers to throw down their
branches.

Act 5, scene 7: *A man of woman born*

Setting: Outside Macbeth's castle, battle raging.

SUMMARY

◆ Macbeth kills young Siward.
◆ Macduff searches for Macbeth.

Macbeth compares himself to a bear tied to a stake. Perhaps
this shows that he now recognizes his 'animal' nature. He
meets and kills the brave but inexperienced Young Siward.

Next Macduff appears, looking for Macbeth. Macduff cannot bring himself to fight hired or forced men with whom he has no personal quarrel. He exits and Malcolm takes the stage with Old Siward. Malcolm notes that some of Macbeth's men have switched sides. There is much entering and exiting, giving an impression of the fast-moving confusion of battle.

Act 5, scene 8: *Grand finale!*

The big climax. Macbeth goes down fighting. In some editions this is part of scene 7.

Setting: The plain outside Macbeth's castle.

SUMMARY

◆ Macduff meets Macbeth. They fight.
◆ Ross announces that young Siward is dead.
◆ Macduff enters with Macbeth's head.
◆ Malcolm announces that he will be crowned.

T*urn, hell-hound, turn*

Macduff tracks down the tyrant. Macbeth at first refuses to fight him, because there is already too much Macduff family blood on his *soul*. Macduff insists and Macbeth warns Macduff that he is wasting his time – he, Macbeth, cannot be killed by any man *of woman born*. Macduff reveals that he was *from his mother's womb/ Untimely ripped*. So, now we know that Macduff can, and probably will, kill Macbeth.

They fight. Now Macbeth can have no real hope of winning the battle. He also knows that he could die at Macduff's hands. Yet he is determined to fight on and not be captured.
○ What do you think of his resolve to *try the last*? Is he a hero?

There is a brief lull in the fighting, as Old Siward hears that his son is dead. The old warrior resigns himself to the news once he knows that his son had *his hurts before* (on the front of his body), showing that he was not running away.

Macbeth dead, Malcolm king

Macduff enters holding Macbeth's head. At the same time he hails Malcolm as king. All join in agreeing. The nation is at last unified.

Malcolm shows that he is going to be a good king by announcing his intention to reward those who have fought on his side and call home those who have been forced to flee abroad. Peace and order are restored, which is how a tragedy has to end.

Hotspot

(Answers on p. 64)

1 Who –
   (a) has *almost forgot the taste of fears*?
   (b) *should have died hereafter*?
   (c) was *Untimely ripped* from his mother's womb?
   (d) had *his hurts before*?
   (e) tells the thanes, *Henceforth be earls*?

2 Match up the evidence with what it shows about each character:
   (a) Macbeth calls for his armour before he needs it, then changes his mind.
   (b) Macbeth begins to be *aweary of the sun.*
   (c) Macduff says *Turn, hell-hound, turn.*
   (d) Macbeth at first will not fight Macduff.
   (e) Malcolm says he will soon *reckon with your several loves.*

   He is generous, wanting to reward those who deserve it.
   He is restless and agitated.
   He still has some conscience.
   He no longer wants to live.
   He is too honourable to stab a man in the back.

3 On a large sheet of paper, make a Mind Map of the three 'M's – Macbeth, Macduff and Malcolm – showing how each is presented in the last four scenes. Add key lines as evidence.

4 How does each image opposite figure in these last four scenes?

No need for you to fight to the bitter end. Take a break!

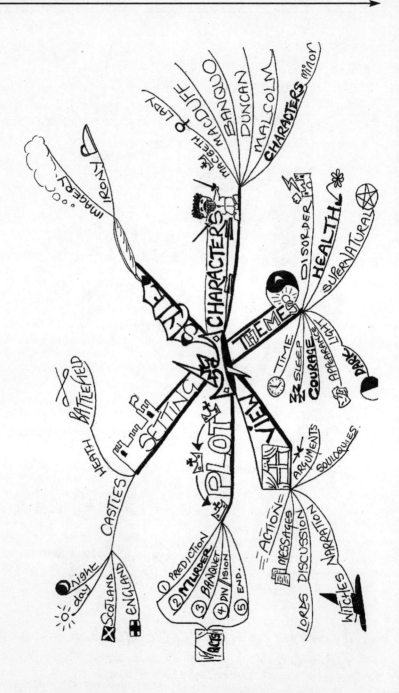

Answers

ACT 1, SCENE 5

Lady Macbeth fears Macbeth's *kindness*. She calls on *spirits* to fill her with *cruelty*. She pictures heaven peeping through a *blanket*. She tells Macbeth to be like a *snake* hiding under a *flower*.

ACT 1, SCENE 7

1 (a) He should be playing host to Duncan.
(b) We'd take our chances in the afterlife – even if it meant going to hell for murder.
(c) Ambition may be his downfall.
(d) Tense uncertainty.
(e) She calls him a coward.

2 Keywords: subject related host ambition good

3 (a) 'You're a coward'; (b) 'You don't love me'; (c) 'If I'd sworn to dash my baby's brains out I would'; (d) 'There's no way we can fail'.

ACT 2, SCENE 1

1 (a) Banquo. When he tries to sleep he worries about the Witches' prophecies.
(b) Banquo. He is uneasy and senses danger.
(c) Macbeth. He cannot tell reality from imagination.
(d) Macbeth fears that words and thought will stop him from taking action.

ACT 2, SCENE 2

1 (a) Lady Macbeth. She has had a drink to steady her nerves.
(b) Lady Macbeth. She knows that if they bungle the murder attempt they are ruined.
(c) Macbeth. He regrets the murder.
(d) Lady Macbeth. She thinks that if they can hide their guilt all will be well. She doesn't consider the effects of a guilty conscience.

ACT 2, SCENE 3

1 (a) Macduff. He is patient and good-humoured.
(b) Macbeth. He is still in shock, and may be afraid that if he says more he will give himself away.

(c) Macduff. He is a man of action, though perhaps too shocked to act usefully.

(d) Lady Macbeth. Her inappropriate reaction shows her guilt. The bad thing is that Duncan has been murdered, not whose house it has happened in.

2 (a) Macduff; (b) Macbeth; (c) Lady Macbeth; (d) Malcolm.

ACT 3, SCENE 4

1 (a) Fleance; (b) Macbeth's; (c) a dagger; (d) a spy; (e) sleep.

ACT 4, SCENE 3

1 Lust, greed and destructiveness.
2 (a) Malcolm knows some men are good.
  (b) Malcolm is cautious about trusting people.
  (c) Macduff is honest, and loyal to Scotland.
  (d) Ross cannot bring himself to break the news.
  (e) Macduff has feelings.

ACT 5, SCENES 5–7

1 (a) Macbeth; (b) Lady Macbeth; (c) Macduff; (d) Young Siward; (e) Malcolm.
2 (a) He is restless and agitated.
  (b) He no longer wants to live.
  (c) He is too honourable to stab a man in the back.
  (d) He still has some conscience.
  (e) He is generous, wanting to reward those who deserve it.
4 (a) Macbeth sees human life as a *brief candle*.
  (b) Macbeth sees himself as a captive bear forced to fight.
  (c) Malcolm's men use branches for camouflage. The Witches said Macbeth was safe until Birnam Wood came to Dunsinane. Now it has.
  (d) Macduff calls Macbeth a *hell-hound* and tells him to turn and face him.
  (e) Macduff kills and beheads Macbeth. The head perhaps represents the 'head' of the country.

M ODEL ANSWER

QUESTION

How does Shakespeare present Macbeth and Lady Macbeth in Act 2, scenes 1 and 2?

Before you begin to write you should think about:

◆ Their different attitudes to the murder.
◆ What they do.
◆ What they say and how they say it.
◆ How their relationship is revealed.

PLAN

◆ Macbeth controlled at first.
◆ 'Dagger' speech; Macbeth not taking responsibility. Grim imagery.
◆ Lady Macbeth alone – bold, uncaring; her father.
◆ Macbeth in shock. The prayers, sleep.
◆ Lady Macbeth practical, takes charge.
◆ Daggers.
◆ 'A little water'; 'seas'.
◆ Coward!

ESSAY

In these scenes Shakespeare presents first Macbeth, then Lady Macbeth, then the two together. In scene 1 Macbeth manages to control himself when talking to Banquo. Although his tone is rather strained, he manages to pretend that everything is all right. However, once he is alone, his deep doubts and fears emerge.[1]

Macbeth's dagger hallucination shows that he is mentally unbalanced. Perhaps this is a vision sent by the Witches, but it is more likely to spring from Macbeth's imagination. Even he wonders if it is 'A dagger of the mind, a false creation' coming from his feverish brain.[2] It seems to lead him towards the murder. This suggests that he is not taking responsibility for what he is about to do.[3]

Macbeth seems very changeable here. One moment he seems to be led by the dagger, and in the next he says 'There's no such thing.' This may be because of his feverish state of mind, which stems from the conflict he feels. He wants to be king, but the idea of murdering Duncan still horrifies him.[4]

The next part of the speech is full of grim imagery pointing to Macbeth's fear and horror. He says that 'Nature seems dead,' which is a frightening idea. He thinks of wicked dreams and witchcraft. He pictures murder as a person whose watchman is the howling wolf, and who strides like Tarquin (a Roman rapist), but also like a ghost, towards the murder. These are images of death, violence and the unknown. Macbeth is so afraid that he even imagines the cobblestones giving away his whereabouts.[5]

Finally he tells himself to stop talking and take action. He is more comfortable with action than with his thoughts.[6]

Shakespeare shows us Macbeth's feelings in scene 1. In scene 2 he contrasts them with Lady Macbeth's.[7] She does not sound horrified or guilty. Instead she sounds as if she revels in the murder. Wine has made her 'bold', and she makes an uncaring joke. She compares the shrieking owl to the man who is giving a 'stern' goodnight by ringing the funeral bell. Her view of Duncan's attendants is scornful and cruel. She does not care whether they live or die.[8] Yet she says that she would have killed Duncan herself had he not reminded her of her own father. This could be a hint of softness, or an excuse.[9]

Macbeth's attitude to the murder is completely different.[10] He already regrets it and says his bloody hands are 'a sorry sight'. Lady Macbeth thinks he is a fool to say so, which is ironic as later in the play she becomes obsessed with a spot of blood she thinks she sees on her own hand. He seems to be in shock. Rather than deciding what to do next, he cannot stop thinking about the murder. He is disturbed by the fact that he could not say 'Amen', like a Christian, to the prayers of Duncan's sons. He has also heard a voice telling him that he has murdered sleep – more evidence of his fearful imagination and deep sense of guilt.[11]

The poetic way in which Macbeth talks about sleep is not very helpful at a time when he should be deciding what to do. Shakespeare contrasts him with his down-to-earth wife when she fails to understand him, and asks, plainly, 'What do you mean?'[12]

Lady Macbeth tells her husband to stop thinking in such a 'brainsickly' way. She also thinks that all they need to do is wash off the blood and pin the blame on the attendants. For her, guilt is not a problem. The only worry is being found out.[13]

Lady Macbeth takes charge of the situation because although Macbeth is normally a man of action, he is now too emotional to act sensibly. She takes the daggers back to the murder scene, showing that she is either brave or unfeeling.[14]

Shakespeare contrasts their attitudes and character using the images of water. Lady Macbeth thinks that they can literally wash their hands of the murder: 'A little water clears us of this deed.' Macbeth feels so guilty that he thinks if he tried to wash his hands in the 'multitudinous seas' the water would turn blood-red rather than making his hands clean. The long words 'multitudinous' and 'incarnadine' suggest the hugeness of his guilt.[15]

Lady Macbeth calls her husband a coward, as she did when she persuaded him to commit the murder. Their relationship has been close, but the murder is already driving them apart. She cannot respect or understand his fear, and he cannot depend on her for emotional support.[16]

WHAT'S SO GOOD ABOUT IT?

1 Good opening points, then moves quickly to the important soliloquy.
2 Good assessment of Macbeth's mental state, based on the evidence.
3 Interesting personal interpretation.
4 Good observation of Macbeth's changing view. Explanation shows understanding.
5 Explains how imagery shows Macbeth's state of mind.
6 Understanding of Macbeth based on the play so far.
7 Awareness of Shakespeare's dramatic technique.
8 Understanding of what Lady Macbeth says and what it shows.
9 Awareness of a character contradiction, and that it could be taken in more than one way.
10 Introduces comparison of attitudes – as suggested by the question notes.
11 Good use of evidence.
12 Awareness of how Macbeth's language shows his state of mind, and how Lady Macbeth's response shows her character. Good use of quotation.
13 Sums up Lady Macbeth's attitude.
14 Awareness of what actions show – following the question notes.
15 Understanding of imagery, and of how Shakespeare's choice of words adds to meaning.
16 Brief conclusion summing up how the murder has affected the relationship.

HINTS ON THE SHAKESPEARE EXAM

Your SATs Shakespeare exam is 1 hour 15 minutes long. You have to answer **one** task on **one** extract from **one** play. The tasks are of three basic types:

1 **Critical**. *Example*: 'What do you learn about Macbeth's changing state of mind from the way he speaks and behaves in this scene?'
2 **Dramatic**. *Example*: 'Imagine you were going to direct this scene for a class performance. Explain how you want the pupil acting the part of Macbeth to show his changing state of mind in this scene.'
3 **In character**. *Example*: 'Imagine you are Lady Macbeth. Write about your thoughts and feelings as you consider the day's events.'

Any one of these types could turn up in the exam.

The critical task

The wording of the task is often open-ended, giving you room to express your views and write about what interests you. There are always hints on what to think about, but you may well think of additional ideas.

Stick to the question. You should also stick to the extract – but you will impress the examiner if you show *relevant* knowledge of the whole play. For example you could say how an idea or line echoes one that comes earlier, or hints at what comes later.

You can give your personal response, and it may get you extra marks, but always support it with evidence. Refer to what a character does (e.g. 'She takes the daggers') or says (e.g. 'She calls him a coward'), or give a direct quote (e.g. 'When she says, "I shame to wear a heart so white," she shows …').

The dramatic task

For this task you must imagine the play performed on stage.
How would it look and sound? Shakespeare himself gave only
very basic **stage directions** (instructions to the actors), so you
can use your imagination a lot. However, you should base
your suggestions on your understanding of the extract, and
give evidence to support your views. For example:

> Lady Macbeth shows her scorn for Macbeth in the line,
> 'Infirm of purpose!'. She should step quickly towards him,
> contrasting her active mood with his. As she says, 'Give me
> the daggers,' she should snatch them angrily to show her
> impatience.

The 'in character' task

For this you must really imagine you are the character. This
can be fun, but you must still base your writing on the
evidence. You do not need to write like Shakespeare, but you
will get marks for a style that convincingly suggests the
character. One good technique is to include short quotations:
'He called his bloody hands "a sorry sight". The fool! Had they
been mine I would have rejoiced!' Try to feel your way into
the part. What do you know about the character? How would
he or she think, feel, speak and move at this point in the play?

Planning and checking

Read the task carefully. If you have studied two extracts, read
both tasks and decide which one to do. Then read the extract
carefully. Don't worry if you can't understand every word. Aim
to get the general sense of the words, and the mood they
suggest.

Use the task hints to help you plan. You could turn each hint
into one branch of a quick Mind Map. Number the branches
to put your ideas in order.

LOSSARY

alliteration   repetition of a sound at the start of a word or syllable; e.g. **d**usty **d**eath.

aside   a short speech spoken without other characters hearing.

back-story   dialogue (conversation), often between minor characters, describing events not acted out in the play, especially before the point at which it starts.

blank verse   the kind of poetic lines that Shakespeare normally uses. Blank verse has five pairs of **syllables** in each line and does not rhyme ('blank = unrhymed).

dramatic irony   when the audience knows something important that at least one character onstage does not know.

imagery   the kind of word pictures a writer uses to make ideas come to life.

images   a writer's word pictures, including **metaphors** and **similes**.

irony   ridiculing an opinion or belief by saying the opposite of what you really mean or pretending not to know the true facts.

metaphor   an **image** in which one thing is described as if it is something else; e.g. Macbeth calls life 'a tale told by an idiot'.

personification   the technique of picturing a thing, or an idea, as if it is a person. The verb is *personify*: 'Shakespeare personifies Murder as …'

soliloquy   a speech spoken by a character alone onstage, thinking aloud.

syllable   the smallest part of a word that you can say. The word *syllable* has three syllables.

tragedy   a play featuring revenge, death and disorder before the **tragic hero** dies and order is restored.

tragic hero   someone basically noble, but who has a fatal weakness or makes a bad mistake. This, combined with fate, leads to the hero's downfall and death.

INDEX

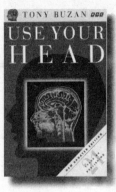

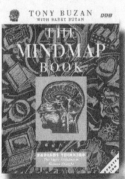